ABANDONED
JACKSON
COUNTY
—OREGON—

ABANDONED JACKSON COUNTY
— OREGON —

TOWNS LOST TO TIME

MARGARET LAPLANTE

AMERICA
THROUGH TIME®
ADDING COLOR TO AMERICAN HISTORY

America Through Time is an imprint of Fonthill Media LLC
www.through-time.com
office@through-time.com

Published by Arcadia Publishing by arrangement with Fonthill Media LLC
For all general information, please contact Arcadia Publishing:
Telephone: 843-853-2070
Fax: 843-853-0044
E-mail: sales@arcadiapublishing.com
For customer service and orders:
Toll-Free 1-888-313-2665

www.arcadiapublishing.com

First published 2021

Copyright © Margaret LaPlante 2021

ISBN 978-1-63499-302-9

Typeset in Mrs Eaves XL Serif Narrow
Printed and bound in England

CONTENTS

A view of Mount McLoughlin and Table Rock.

A sawmill in front of Table Rock.

Acknowledgments

This book would not be possible without the generosity of the following who allowed me to use their historic photographs: Evelyn Williams, the Gold Hill Museum, the Gold Hill Historical Society, the Phoenix Museum, the Phoenix Historical Society, the Woodville Museum, the Woodville Historical Society, the Eagle Point Museum, the Eagle Point Historical Society, the Trail Creek Tavern Museum, and Upper Rogue Historical Society.

A bridge over the Rogue River.

The Rogue River.

INTRODUCTION

Long before the first pioneers settled in Jackson County, tribes of Native Americans called this part of Southern Oregon home. The majority of the local Native Americans were of the Takelma tribe. From time to time, a fur trapper or explorer would pass through the area, but for the most part they were undisturbed. One group of French fur trappers found the Takelmas to be rather troublesome and referred to them as "La Riviere aux Coquins," or rogues. Soon the valley became known as the Rogue Valley.

The Takelmas felled sugar pine trees and used the wood for their "Pitt homes." They dug into the ground 18-24 inches along the perimeters of the house. They erected posts in the corners, then used the planks of the sugar pine for the siding. The roofs were made from either sugar pine or other natural resources.

The Takelmas women wore knee-length deerskin shirts adorned with fringe of white grass. The men wore deerskin shirts and leggings tied with a belt, deerskin robes, and blankets and hats made from deerskin or bearskin. They lined their moccasins with grass or fur. During the cold months, they wore sleeves made from fox skins. They embellished their garments with abalone and other shells, white grass braids, and buckskin tassels.

They wove baskets from tree roots, vines, and other natural resources. The baskets were used for food gathering, food preparation, and serving. They also wove baskets to carry their infants.

The diet of the Takelma Indians consisted of sugar pine nuts and the bark from the sugar pine tree, wild berries and plums, seeds from other trees and plants, and edible plants that grew naturally. They would shell acorns then mash them using a mortar and pestle. They would then place the mashed acorns on clean sand and pour hot water over them to leach them. That process was repeated, then the mixture was boiled by placing it into a tightly woven basket filled with water and heating it over hot stones. Camas bulbs were baked in a pit dug in the ground. They would place alder bark between the hot stones in the pit and the bulbs. They would cook the bulbs for a day or two until they were roasted. They could then mash them into cakes and store them for the cold months. In addition to hunting deer and elk, the river and creeks provided an abundance of salmon and trout. The Indians kept an eye on Mount McLoughlin, and when the snow melted to the point that angel wings appeared, they knew the Rogue River would be teaming with salmon. Trading with other tribes that passed through the area allowed the Indians to obtain unique items that were not available to them locally.

The Takelma Indians lived a peaceful existence but things changed drastically when the California Gold Rush and the Donation Land Claim Act bought thousands of pioneers across the plains, many of whom settled in the Rogue Valley. Whether the Pioneers came overland or traveled by sea going around the Horn, it was a very long and difficult journey. Some came for the gold, some for the land, but they all came in search of a better life.

The decision to begin a new life in Oregon was not taken lightly. Preparing for the journey could take up to a year. Heading out west either by way of the Horn or across the plains meant leaving your family behind, knowing that you would probably never see them again. Sometimes two or three generations of families traveled together but others set off alone. Either way the pioneers traveled as a group; it wasn't unusual to have forty to fifty wagons in the wagon train. Those traveling overland left from "jump off points" in Missouri. Those towns were well equipped to provide any last-minute supplies needed and that is where the wagon train would form. It was important to leave early in the spring to ensure they would arrive before the first winter storms.

For those who came overland, it was a 2,000-mile walk through rain, heat, wind, and dust. Water along the way was a mixed blessing. It quenched their thirst, but it was also the cause of numerous deaths along the way from cholera. It wasn't just the water that cost so many pioneers their lives. There were accidents and diseases that many pioneers succumbed to. Those who died on the trail were buried where they died. The next day the family had to continue on, leaving their loved one behind in a shallow grave.

Food could be scarce along the way. Sometimes there was good hunting and fishing, but other times the pioneers had to rely on what they had brought. Coffee was an important part of each meal as it helped to mask the taste of the water, which was sometimes muddy and polluted. The women made biscuits, cornbread, muffins, and bread either inside or on top of their Dutch oven. They also cooked bacon, beans, fresh meat, or fish in the Dutch ovens. Some pioneers travelled with chickens in cages that hung from the back of their wagon, thus giving them fresh eggs. Others brought cows so they would have milk and butter. They found that by strapping the butter churn to the side of the wagon, they would have butter by the end of the day, because the rough terrain did the churning for them. If they had had any success at hunting, they would hang the meat from the wagon to cure it.

The pioneers encountered many Indians on their journey overland. Most of the Indians were very friendly and helpful, but as time went by and the Indian's natural resources began disappearing due to the heavy wagon traffic, tensions ran high in certain areas. There was always a language barrier, but the pioneers and the Indians learned certain signals to communicate with one another. Many Indians used their river skills and for a fee would help the pioneers cross the rivers.

William Hoffman came overland in 1853 with his wife, Caroline, their six daughters, his two sisters, and his brother-in-law. He described some of the hardships in his journal:

Monday June 27th 1853

We got up this morning at half past seven & traveled over a heavy sandy road until 12 o'clk when we stopped to noon near the river. The wind soon raised to a gale from the west and blew so fiercely that it was deemed impracticable to go forward on account of the clouds of dust & sand. We came about 10 miles at noon. The wind storm continued so severe until night that we were compelled to remain in camp until next morning. Fortunately our cattle had pretty fair grazing in the River bottom.

Saturday June 25th 1853

We remained in camp until 3 o'clk for the purpose of enabling the women to wash & bake. We then traveled until 8 O'Clk P.M. before we could encamp. The mosquitoes were exceedingly bad causing our cattle to leave the encampment unperceived, which caused no little excitement & there was a general rush for horses to go in pursuit, the cattle finding their tormentors everywhere, returned into camp in half an hour. We were compelled to chain up our cattle for the night. The Road traveled this afternoon was exceedingly heavy, traveled about 5 miles.

Friday June 10th 1853

We started this morning at 5 O'Clk and encamped for breakfast about nine. Started again at 11 O'Clk. Here we leave the little Blue and cross over to the Platte a distance of 25 miles without wood & but little water. We arrived at 12 Mile creek about half past three o'clk. The water is quite muddy, not fit even for cattle. Traveled about three miles farther and encamped for the night having traveled 18 or 20 miles to day. A severe storm of wind & rain came on soon after we encamped. There is almost constant wind on the Plains which modifies the heat, which would otherwise be almost unbearable.

Americus Savage brought his wife, Mary and their four children overland in 1851. By October they had arrived in Oregon but were still traveling in their covered wagon in search of the area they wanted to settle. He wrote in his journal:

06 Oct 1851

On the sixth of October about 11 o'clock Mary gave birth to a son. It was raining hard, everything was drenched with the cold rain. I covered the wagon with quilts and warmed it with pans of live coals and made everything as comfortable for two days as possible and in that time moved six miles to a house we had rented and would have got into sooner had my cattle come as had expected. In a few days Mary was up full of courage and ambition, ready to take charge of the children while I went out to work. I found myself in a new country with new prospects, in my prime with a stout heart, and a willing mind ready to do all I could for the welfare of my little family and my Mary. I had nothing left but one yoke of oxen. I had to sell two yoke to pay our passage down the river and other debts.

For some pioneers, once they reached Oregon, they thought the worst was behind them, only to discover that new challenges lay ahead. Elizabeth Dixon Smith Geer came overland in 1847. She wrote in her diary:

November 18

My husband is sick. It rains and snows. We start around the falls this morning with our wagons. We have five miles to go. I carry my babe and lead, or rather carry another, through snow, mud, and water almost to my knees. It is the worst road a team could possibly travel. I went ahead with my children and I was afraid to look behind me for fear of seeing the wagons overturn into the mud and water with everything in them. My children gave out with cold and fatigue and could not travel, and the boys had to unhitch the oxen and bring them and carry the children on to camp. I was so cold and numb that I could not tell by the feeling that I had any feet. We started this morning at sunrise and did not camp until after dark, and there was not one dry thread on one of us—not even on the babe. I had carried my babe and I was so fatigued that I could scarcely speak or step. When I got here I found my husband lying in Welch's wagon very sick. He had brought Mrs. Polk down the day before and was taken sick. We had to stay up all night for our wagons were left halfway back. I have not told half we suffered. I am not adequate to the task.

February 2

To-day we buried my earthly companion. Now I know what none but widows know: that is, how comfortless is a widow's life; especially when left in a strange land without money or friends, and the care of seven children.

In Jackson County, James Poole and James Cluggage are credited with discovering gold during the winter of 1851-1852. It wasn't long before others learned of the discovery and flocked to the area. The early settlers named the county after President Andrew Jackson who served from 1829-1837.

Within months, Jackson County began to take shape. Towns began springing up complete with churches, stores and schools. Some of the pioneers worked mining for gold, others ran pack trains bringing in supplies, some did construction work, operated mills, opened stores, taught school, or began farming or ranching.

A view of Mount McLoughlin.

A view of Crater Lake in the winter.

Rogue Valley pear orchards in front of Mount McLoughlin.

1

ABANDONED

Some of Jackson County's early towns survived, others were left abandoned. Families moved away seeking better opportunities. Homes, schools, churches, and stores were left behind to crumble to the ground.

In addition to the towns mentioned in this book, there were other small towns or areas that are not featured due to a lack of existing information and photographs to document their existence. Examples include Asbestos, Draper, Dudley, Leeds, Peyton, Siskiyou, Wellen, Persist, Pinehurst, Provolt, and Soda Springs.

Houses that were once filled with laughter and stories were left abandoned.

This abandoned barn was once an integral part of a family farm but was left to fall to the ground.

The Kubli Store complete with a waterwheel are shown *circa* 1946. When this photograph was taken, it had been decades since the last customer had walked through the doors of the store.

2

APPLEGATE VALLEY

The Applegate Valley is named after Jesse and Lindsay Applegate, two brothers who came overland with their families in 1843. This was years before the Great Migration which brought thousands of pioneers across the Plains.

The brothers had been intrigued with the prospect of traveling overland ever since meeting Captain Clark of the famed Lewis and Clark Expedition. They had also met William Price Hunt who had led an overland expedition to the mouth of the Columbia River for John Jacob Astor.

In May of 1843, the Applegate family, consisting of three brothers—Lindsay, Jesse, and Charles—along with their wives and children, set out for Oregon. They joined approximately 800 men, women, and children traveling in 100 wagons that left from Independence, Missouri.

When they reached Fort Walla Walla, they were advised to leave their wagons and animals with the Hudson Bay Company at the fort. There were no boats to be found, so they built three makeshift boats out of driftwood. Dr. Marcus Whitman found Indians who agreed to help pilot the crafts down the river. During a bad stretch of the Columbia River the boat capsized. Jesse's son Edward, age ten, and Lindsay's son Warren, age nine, and a family friend, age seventy, all died in this accident.

In 1846, the U.S. government asked the Applegate brothers and Levi Scott to find a better route leading into Oregon that would not involve the treacherous Snake and Columbia Rivers. They set out to blaze a trail into Southern Oregon, and thus the Applegate Trail, also known as the Southern Route, came to be. Over the years, thousands of immigrants followed the Southern Route on the final leg of their journey to Oregon.

Today many people make their home in the beautiful Applegate Valley. However, few areas in Jackson County have seen as many changes as the Applegate Valley over the years. Many of the early towns cease to exist; two of the towns are actually underneath Applegate Lake.

Before there were any foot bridges in the area, a tramway was used to get from Adelbert McKee's property to Beaver Creek School on the other side of the river. A cable was suspended across the river. The cable was secured to trees and anchored to boulders. The box was large enough for four people. The cables were pulled by hand. Teacher Maud Harr and her students Orpha Lewis and Aletha Buck are pictured.

There were two rope-and-pulley aerial tramways across the Applegate River. Pictured is teacher Ina Stoker preparing for her commute to school.

The town of Watkins was named for Mark Watkins, who arrived in the 1850s and worked as a miner and a farmer in the area. The town of Watkins is now under the Applegate Lake. Pictured at Watkins School in 1892 are standing back row: teacher Mary Bedford, A. E. Collins, Emma Bedford, Mathilda Smith, Laura Dorn, Maria Watkins, and John Collings. The middle row includes: Winnie McLaren, Edith Worthington, Irene Smith, Minnie Watkins, and Ollie McLaren. Seated: William Smith, Robert Watkins, Frank Collings, Zeb J. Collings, Willie McLaren, and Carrie Dorn.

Teacher Roseltha Birchard is pictured in 1907 with her students at Watkins School.

These students are pictured in front of Watkins School in 1910. Teacher Emma Wendt is shown with Ernest Dorn, ? Collins, Katherine Byrne, Grace Harr, Mamie Watkins, ? Moses, Pearl Watkins, and Helen O'Brien.

Teacher Emma Wendt prepares for her day teaching at Watkins School.

The Watkins School is pictured *circa* 1926.

Students on their way to Watkins School on a swinging foot bridge.

The Sterling Mine is shown. Sterlingville was named for James Sterling who is credited with being the first to discover gold in the creek. He was a pioneer from Illinois who settled in Eden Precinct. While prospecting, he came across the creek and discovered gold. He returned to Eden Precinct to gather his supplies. Somehow word leaked out and by the time he returned to the creek, every inch had been claimed. He left the area having never mined at his namesake creek. He lived out his days in California.

OPPOSITE PAGE:

Above: In 1924, a new building was constructed for Watkins School. Pictured in 1929 are standing: Pearl Whitney, ?, ? DeWolf, Guy and Polly Watkins, and Mamie Winningham. Seated: Valera Winningham, ?, Louise Harr, Violet and Ruth Whitney.

Below: Melvin Arnold and his family are pictured in front of what remained of Watkins School before it was torn down.

Piping at the Sterling Mine.

OPPOSITE PAGE:

Above: By 1854, Sterlingville had a hotel, a bakery, and a general store. A school was established in 1869. The Sterlingville School is pictured *circa* 1917. By 1939, there were not enough students to warrant keeping the school open. The remaining students were sent to the school in Ruch. The area of Sterlingville still exists, but there is no longer an actual town.

Below: Gold miners used the term "steamboated" to indicate that a gold mine had been worked out or did not meet expectations. There was a town in the Applegate Valley named Steamboat. Pictured in front of their home in Steamboat in the 1890s are George and Permelia Culy with their children: Branch, Neldrett, Lora, and Cary. The Steamboat Post Office was located inside their home for a period of time.

George Culy petitioned the Jackson County Superintendent of Schools for a schoolhouse to serve the children in Steamboat. The petition was granted in 1889. The school was located on the Culy's property. The teacher pictured is Maude Harr.

Teacher Nettie Lewis Thompson is pictured (left) in front of the Steamboat School *circa* 1903. Branch Culy is standing in front of the teacher. In the back row: Ned Culy, Dan Shearer, Lucy Shearer, and Lora Culy. Seated: Frank Culy, Frank and Harold Loosely.

Teacher Mabel Thompson is pictured in 1912 at the Beaver Creek School. The students pictured include: Fern Phillips, Orpha Lewis, Luella ?, Doris McKee, Merritt Dews, Lydia Stephenson, Emmett Phillips, Omar Culy, Dorothy McKee, Helen Culy, Orie Phillips, and Earl Stephenson.

Some of the students pictured in front of the Beaver Creek School are Luella McKee, Dorris McKee, Fern Phillips, Ora Phillips, Vern Stephenson, Homer Stephenson, Leonard McKee, Letha Buck, Orpha Lewis, Lydia Lewis, Harold Bostwick, Floyd McKee, Clarence Buck, and teacher Maude Harr.

Students at Beaver Creek School include: William Dietrick, Thelma Childers, Evelyn Childers, Omar Culy, Lydia Lewis, Helen Culy, Dorothy McKee, Clara McKee, Emmett Phillips, Orie Phillips, Earl Stephenson, and Lou Culy.

The community gathered to watch the Beaver Creek School's Thanksgiving Pageant in 1932. Included in the picture are: ? Lewis, Douglas McKee, Victor Anderson, Clara Faye McKee, Rosella Offenbacher, Marcene McKee, and Evelyn Byrne.

Students at Beaver Creek School in 1933 include front row: Evelyn Byrne, Grace Moore, Rosella Offenbacher, Carmoleta Lewis, Clara Faye McKee and Marcene McKee. The back row include: Shirley Ann Crosby, Audrey Fletcher, Frances Port, Vonetta Rupretch, Gladys Byrne, and Shirley Lewis.

This sign on Highway 238 points to the town of Copper. Today the town of Copper is under the Applegate Lake. In 1976, the U.S. government purchased the land from the homeowners and began construction of the Applegate Dam. The U.S. Army Corp of Engineers oversaw the private construction companies involved in the project. By the end of the project, a total of 4,481 troy ounces of gold and 589 ounces of silver were removed. The contractors and the U.S. government shared in the sale of the gold and silver. The dam was completed in 1980.

The town of Copper came to life in the 1890s when a group of miners searching for gold discovered copper deposits. The Blue Ledge Mine pictured employed many people for years.

William and Margaret Thompson are pictured with Mr. Waley and two unknown gentlemen at the Blue Ledge Mine in 1906.

William Thompson on left, Mr. Waley in center, and unknown on right at the Blue Ledge Mine in 1906. After the last of the copper was mined, people stayed in the area, making a living ranching and farming.

The children pictured here are in front of the Uniontown School. Todd and Robert Cameron were pioneers who came overland in 1852. They began mining but later found more success at farming. Todd moved to Sterlingville and opened a bakery. Next, he bought some land nearby and opened a store. Although the Civil War was far from Oregon, both Todd and Robert felt strong ties to the North and named their new town Uniontown. Eventually Uniontown just faded away as the residents moved on.

A new Uniontown School was constructed in the 1920s. This photograph was taken in 1936.

Teacher Ailene Inlow is pictured in front of Uniontown School.

Pictured is the Drake School. In 1913, construction began on a new school and it opened the following year as the Ruch School.

The new Ruch School is pictured on May 16, 1914. The town of Ruch was named for Casper (Cap) Ruch. His parents were immigrants from Switzerland who arrived in America in the 1860s and came overland. In 1896 Casper bought 10 acres of land near present-day Highway 238 and Little Applegate Road. He opened a mercantile store and a blacksmith shop and built a home nearby. In 1897, Casper became postmaster and named the town Ruch.

Applegate School *circa* 1902.

This photograph of the Applegate School was taken in 1913. The bricks for the school were made from clay that was adjacent to the school.

Teacher Thelma Stringer is pictured with her students in 1938 at the Applegate School. Back row: Silas Davis, Fritz Offenbacher, Georgia Benedict, Lorraine Rowden, Billie Boussun, Jack Richie, Charles Rolls, Eleanor Corbin, and LaDonna Gibson. Front row: Beverly Surran, Davy Crenshaw, Dickie Francis, Gary Denzer, Barbara Rolls, Temple Rose, Jimmie Hanshon, Richard Huggins, Leonard Corbin, Harriet Taylor, and Betty Jean Studebaker.

Mary and Meada Winningham and Ella Horn are pictured in front of the Forest Creek School.

The area of Forest Creek still exists, but the actual town is just a memory. Forest Creek School, pictured here, closed in 1945.

Logtown was named for Frank Logg, who was an early pioneer. He found an ideal spot along the road where pack trains travelled between Jacksonville and Crescent City. He set up camp and began mining for gold. It wasn't long before others joined him and soon Logtown boasted saloons, a bakery, a livery, and a blacksmith shop. Today all that is left of Logtown is the cemetery.

John and Maryum McKee were early pioneers who came across the plains. Maryum brought a slip of a yellow rose with her from Missouri and planted it on their Donation Land Claim in what became known as Logtown. The Logtown cemetery was on the McKee's Donation Land Claim. More than 150 years later, cuttings from that rose bloom all over the Rogue Valley as well as at the Logtown Cemetery.

Missouri Flat was originally in Jackson County. Years later the boundary was changed to Josephine County. The cemetery is located on Kubli Road. The road was named for Kasper Kubli, an early pioneer. Kasper immigrated from Switzerland in 1852. In 1853, he arrived in the Applegate Valley and found success mining, farming, stock raising, and operating a store. Missouri Flat was named by early pioneers who were reminded of their homeland in Missouri. A town sprang up during the gold mining days, but today all that remains is the cemetery.

Cinnabar Springs was located in the Applegate Valley. Cinnabar Springs brought people from all over to experience the spring water that was touted to cure blood diseases and rheumatism. At its height, Cinnabar Springs had a hotel, dance hall, campgrounds, restaurant, and a boarding house. Edward and Edith Kubli are pictured on the far right.

To truly take a step back in time, one can visit the ghost town of Buncom in the Applegate Valley. Three buildings remain—a cookhouse, a post office, and a bunkhouse. Buncom never had the amenities that the nearby towns had such as saloons, hotels, churches, or schools. However, it was home to many miners who worked in the nearby mines.

3

TOLO TO WOODVILLE

A drive through the back roads of Jackson County can reveal names that evoke curiosity. Sometimes there is a random sign but nothing else to connect it to an actual town that once existed. There are signs that have the words Tolo and Dardanelles, but there is nothing else to indicate that these were once vibrant towns. Other times one can come across a name on an old cemetery without realizing that there was once a town that shared the name of the cemetery. Such is the case of the Rock Point Cemetery, the Antioch Cemetery, and the Woodville Cemetery.

Near present-day Central Point, there were the towns of Manzanita and Willow Springs. The Willow Spring School is pictured here on March 6, 1907.

This cattle drive is going through the town of Tolo. The town of Tolo was located between Gold Hill and Woodville.

Pictured is the Tolo covered bridge.

Tolo Falls in front of the Table Rocks.

OPPOSITE PAGE:

Above: Pictured is the Tolo Brick Company. Many of the bricks they manufactured are still in use today in houses, schools, and commercial buildings.

Below: The workers at the Tolo Brick Company are making bricks for a new school in Woodville *circa* 1909-1910.

The Table Rocks are pictured. During World War II, the U.S. government needed additional petroleum for the war effort. They authorized four new shipyards. The shipyards were tasked with building 480 oil tankers. One of the new shipyards was the Kaiser Swan Island Shipyard in Portland. Two of the fuel tankers that were built at the Kaiser Swan Island Shipyard were named for the Rogue Valley: the Jacksonville and the Table Rocks. The Jacksonville was struck by enemy fire in Europe. The Table Rocks survived the war and was sent to Canada to haul iron ore and grain.

Top of next page: Pictured is the Pankey School in Sams Valley *circa* 1910-1911. James Pankey and his family were early settlers to the area and donated part of their land for a school house in 1877. Sams Valley was originally named Moonville after an early settler, Andrew Moon. The name was changed to Sams Valley in honor of Chief Sam. Chief Sam was instrumental in signing the peace treaty that ended the Rogue River Indian War.

The Rock Point Stage Stop is pictured *circa* 1898. Rock Point was located north of Gold Hill. Although it has been more than a century since the last stagecoach came by, the building is still in use today. The Rock Point cemetery is nearby.

A sign boasting that Rock Point had one of the first telegraphs in Jackson County.

This is an early day photograph of the Rock Point bridge. School Superintendent William Colvig once tripped over a cow while walking across the bridge at night. The cow was startled and jumped up, tossing Mr. Colvig into another sleeping cow. Mr. Colvig was not injured but decided he would carry a lantern the next time he had to walk across the bridge which he described "as dark as a stack of black cats in a dark alley."

Camping at Rock Point amongst the pine trees was a favorite pastime.

The town of Rock Point against a backdrop of mountains.

The new Rock Point bridge is pictured. When it was built in 1919, it was touted as having state-of-the-art construction. It was located just downstream from the old bridge. The old bridge was demolished in 1920.

The town of Dardanelles was across the Rogue River from Gold Hill. Shown is an early day schoolhouse in Dardanelles.

Dardanelles School over the years.

The Bybee Springs Hotel was located near Woodville. It was a popular health resort. In addition to the hotel, there were cottages and tents on the property for the guests.

The town of Woodville was named after John Wood, a pioneer of the area. In 1912, the town changed the name to Rogue River in order to capitalize on this resource. They promoted the river for its abundant fishing and recreational opportunities.

The Woodville School was constructed in 1883. The first teacher was W. J. Stanley. This photograph was taken in 1890. The teacher pictured is E. E. Phipps.

Teacher Lincoln Savage is pictured with his students at Woodville School in 1898. Some of the students include: Jimmie Leslie, Grace Bedford, Maggie Smithline, Madge Owings, Abbie Griffin, ? Stevens, ? Connelly, Garfield Osborn, Harvey Bedford, Al Smithline, Carlos Magerle, Will Payburn, Minnie Train, Edna Carter, Coralie Wimer, Lizzie White, Carrie Smithline, Mary Bull, Ruby Bedford, Nellie Magerle, Addie Jones, Anna White, Lula McCord, Myrtle Williams, Rose White, Raymond Stevens, Jeff Wimer, Willie Burkhart, Grace Hullen, John Bull, Myrtle Carter, Mary Hullen, Mary Jones, Pearl Smithline, Grace Stevens, Olie Bull, Charles White, Clarence Wilcox, Ada May Smithline, Charles Hullen, Claude and Joe Burkhart.

These women are enjoying a walk in Woodville. Pictured: Angie Wilcox with her son Lester, Bessie Raminger, Gladys Hamen, Rena Pyburn Whipple with Alice, and Lillian Pyburn Wright with Hazel.

Pictured is the Waldorf Hotel in Woodville *circa* 1911. An article ran on August 01, 1911, in the *Rogue River Courier*; "Mr. T. H. B. Taylor is building a hotel on his property here. The Waldorf will be torn down when the new building is completed. We almost regret to see the old landmark go as it was the first building in Woodville and when used as a stage house, it gave shelter to many noted people."

The town of Woodville is shown in the distance. An article ran in December 1910 in the *Medford Mail Tribune* stating, "Now that we have a new bank and new furniture store with a drug store in sight, Woodville is enjoying a business boom. There are several parties thinking of coming here and investing or going into business."

When this photograph was taken, Woodville only delivered mail to those who lived in the outlining areas. In 1909, only the towns of Grants Pass and Ashland had city mail delivery services. Even Medford was deemed too small to warrant city delivery in 1909. For those who lived in town, they had to walk to the post office to collect their mail.

There was a time that this footbridge in Woodville was the only way to cross the Rogue River.

In 1909, a new steel bridge was constructed at a cost of $14,500.

The new Woodville school is pictured.

The new school and church *circa* 1910.

On September 13, 1911, the *Medford Mail Tribune* reported, "The old Soldiers and Sailors Association of southern Oregon composed of veterans of the Civil War are encamped at Woodville in annual session. Veterans, their wives, children, and grandchildren, assembled in numbers and Woodville's hospitality is being enjoyed by all the visitors."

These horses are hauling logs to a sawmill in Woodville *circa* 1911.

4

FORT LANE, CAMP BAKER AND CAMP WHITE

Jackson County has a very impressive military history. From the earliest war, the Rogue River Indian War in the 1850s, all the way through World War II, Jackson County has figured prominently.

The Rogue River Indian War began when tensions started rising between the new settlers and the Indians. The Indians resented the erosion of the land they had called home for many years. Their hunting, fishing, and natural vegetation suffered, and they began to strike back. Some of the pioneers built blockades around their homes and offered their neighbors a place to stay until the fighting subsided. It wasn't long before an actual war was at hand.

In 1853, tensions had escalated to the point that the Territorial Governor of Oregon sent General Joseph Lane to Jackson County to help both parties reach a peaceful agreement. Captain James W. Nesmith accompanied General Lane and a dozen other men on the journey. He later wrote about the experience saying:

> After a toilsome march, dragging the howitzer and other materials of war through the Umpqua Canyon and up and down the mountain trails made slippery by recent rains, we arrived at General Lane's encampment on [the] Rogue River.

General Lane made arrangements to meet with the Indians at their encampment below the Table Rocks on September 10, 1853. The agreement was that General Lane could bring ten of his men, all unarmed, to meet with the Indians and their Chiefs: Old Jo, John, and Sam. General Lane addressed the Indians by saying:

> I promised in good faith to come into your camp, with ten unarmed men to secure peace. Myself and men are placed in your power, I do not believe that you are such cowardly dogs as to take advantage of our unarmed condition. I know that you can murder us

and you can do so as quickly as you please, but what good will our blood do you? Our murder will exasperate our friends and your tribe will be hunted from the face of the earth. Let us proceed with the treaty, and in place of war, have a lasting peace.

A peace treaty was signed on that day.

A fort was built at the base of the Table Rock Mountains. It was named for General Lane and consisted of a number of buildings to house Captain A. J. Smith and his men. The men were charged with keeping the peace between the parties. All was fine in the beginning, but 1854 saw a few squirmishes. The following year peace gave way and scores of men, women, and children lost their lives on both sides. In October 1856, the government ordered that all Indians be removed to the Siletz Reservation in Lincoln County.

Although the Civil War took place far from Jackson County, the residents followed the news back east. They became increasing concerned about what was happening and decided to open an encampment in Jackson County. In December 1861, Camp Baker opened on the outskirts of Phoenix. Eighty men served under Captain T. S. Harris and were charged with keeping the peace while tensions ran high in Jackson County regarding the Civil War. Camp Baker was named for Edward D. Baker, an Oregon Senator who had been killed at the battle of the Ball's Bluff two months prior. A mounted group known as the Jackson Rangers led by Sewell Traux augmented the Baker Guards.

In the early part of 1941, Jackson County sent promotional material to the U.S. government in the hopes of being selected for a military cantonment. Within days of the Pearl Harbor attack, the U.S. government selected Jackson County for a military cantonment. They chose an area in the Agate Desert where present-day White City is located. They needed 50,000 acres of land for the cantonment. It was decided that the nearby town of Beagle would have to be bulldozed in order to have enough acreage for an artillery range.

The town of Beagle was named for William Beagle. He was a Civil War veteran who came overland with his family in 1872. In 1942, the U.S. Government informed the residents of Beagle that their land was needed for Camp White's artillery range. They were asked to sign a warranty deed giving the U.S. government their property in exchange for $48 an acre. The government came in and bulldozed houses, tore down fences and filled in wells. After World War II ended, the residents were offered the chance to purchase their land back for $48 an acre. Some did return and rebuilt. Those who returned stayed in touch with the residents who chose not to return. They met for annual picnics for the next five decades.

Today all that remains of Fort Lane is a monument erected by the Crater Lake Chapter of the Daughters of the American Revolution.

Camp Baker is pictured.

Construction of Camp White began on January 17, 1942. Camp White was located in present-day White City in the Agate Desert.

Gigantic light towers run by gasoline generators were used during the night so that construction crews could work twenty-four hours a day. Equipment was brought in from out of state. Workers lived on site in "tent cities" consisting of a wood floor with wood sides and a tarp overhead. Local residents were asked to rent out any extra space they had to accommodate workers.

Construction was completed in six months. The first troops of the 91st Fir Tree Division arrived in the summer of 1942. Camp White was officially dedicated on September 15, 1942. It was named for Major General George A. White, who commanded the 41st Infantry Division of the Oregon National Guard from 1930-1941.

More than 40,000 soldiers trained at Camp White. The 91st Division was designated as a triangular division, meaning that the infantry, artillery, medical staff, and engineers were all under one commander. The division was originally activated in 1917 at Fort Lewis, Washington, prior to World War I. Their slogan was "Powder River, Let'er Buck." Their emblem was a western fir tree.

An article ran in *Time Magazine* stating that Camp White was the "Alcatraz of training camps" under the guidance of Major General Charles Gerhardt. Major General Gerhardt fought in World War I. He was quoted as saying, "I purpose to make this 91st Division the best the United States has ever seen."

Not only did the troops train in the icy cold Rogue River, they hiked in sweltering heat, they climbed the Table Rocks, and they slept in pup tents in the rain.

The nurses who trained at Camp White were from the 79th General Hospital Army Nurse Corps. They had already graduated from civilian nursing school and were sent to Camp White to train in military procedures prior to being sent overseas. The nurses learned how to fire a gun, apply a gas mask, march in formation, hike as far as Eagle Point and back, and crawl on their stomachs under barbed wire as practice bullets flew overhead.

In September 1942, General Gerhardt decided that since his troops were of the 91st Infantry, they should hike 91 miles across the rough terrain of Jackson County. More than 2,000 men hiked for five days, averaging fifteen miles per day. The hike ended in Medford where cheering crowds lined Main Street.

In 1942, the U.S. government began detaining Germans as Prisoners of War (POWs.) Sixteen hundred Germans were held at Camp White. The facility had several compounds including barracks, a mess hall, storage buildings and offices. In 1943, the government decided that the POWs could work in industries that did not compete with American workers. Many of the POWs worked in the local orchards and were paid 80 cents per day.

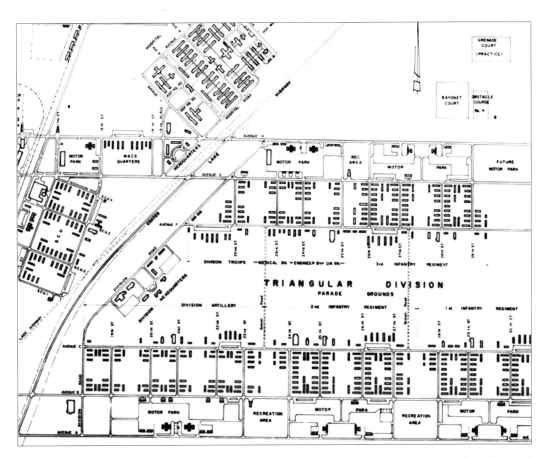

In 1946, the U.S. Government's War Assets Administration placed Camp White on the surplus list and ordered that 1,185 of the buildings be auctioned. They also put the electrical, plumbing, heating, refrigeration systems, and office furniture on the auction block. Many of the buildings were sold locally and used for homes and businesses. A small percentage of the original buildings remain at the Camp White site and have served various purposes over the years.

The town of Antioch was located near Sams Valley in the shadow of the Table Rocks. The Donegan family donated part of their land for a cemetery and a school. When Camp White was built, the government needed the land where the Antioch cemetery was located for their firing range. They laid the headstones flat and placed a foot of sand followed by five feet of dirt over each gravesite. In 1948, the headstones were placed upright.

Pictured is one of the pillboxes, AKA bunkhouses, the military used for their training at Camp White, where the town of Beagle was located.

5

THE UPPER ROGUE VALLEY

The roads leading through the Upper Rogue have been traversed by countless people since the first discovery of Crater Lake. A group of pioneers consisting of John Hillman, Isaac G. Skeeters, Mr. Dodd, James L. Loudon, Patrick McManus, George Ross, and Henry Klippel were amongst the first pioneers to document their discovery of what became known as Crater Lake. John Hillman wrote:

On the evening of the first day, while riding up a long, sloping mountain, we suddenly came in sight of water, and were very much surprised, as we did not expect to see any lakes, and did not know but what we had come in sight of, and close to Klamath Lake, and not until my mule stopped within a few feet of the rim of Crater Lake did I look down, and if I had been riding a blind mule I firmly believe I would have ridden over the edge to death and destruction. We came to the lake a very little to the right of a small sloping butte or mountain, situated in the lake, with a top somewhat flattened. Every man of the party gazed with wonder at the sight before him, and each in his own peculiar way gave expression to the thoughts within him, but we had no time to lose, and after rolling some boulders down the side of the lake, we rode to the left, as near the rim as possible, past the butte, looking to see an outlet for the lake, but we could find none. I was very anxious to find a way to the water, which was immediately vetoed by the whole party, and as the leader of the Californians had become discouraged, we decided to return to camp; but not before we discussed what name we should give the lake. There were many names suggested, but Mysterious Lake and Deep Blue Lake were most favorably received, and on a vote, Deep Blue Lake was chosen for a name.

The Agate School and the Agate Post Office are pictured. Although the area was never an actual desert, it was not prime agriculture land. It was named for the amount of agate, jasper and other minerals located there. During World War II, Camp White occupied part of the Agate Desert. Today, White City occupies part of the Agate Desert.

The Christmas flood of 1964 brought many changes to Jackson County. One of the changes was to build a dam north of Shady Cove to prevent future floods. In building the dam, the towns of Laurelhurst and McLeod were covered by what became Lost Creek Lake. At a depth of 280 feet, it is hard to imagine that there were once communities under Lost Creek Lake.

The Aiken sawmill is pictured. It produced a tremendous amount of lumber that is still in use in homes and businesses in Jackson County.

Opposite page:

Above: The Laurelhurst covered bridge is pictured. The U.S. Government bought the land from the residents of Laurelhurst and McLeod. Construction of the dam began in 1972 and was completed in 1977.

Below: Harvey Deskins is pictured with his family. He established the town of Deskins in 1882. He later sold his land to Squire Aiken, who renamed the town Prospect.

The town of Prospect and the Prospect school are pictured.

Henry Brown is pictured. He and his brothers were early settlers to the Upper Rogue area. They took out Donation Land Claims and named the area Brownsborough, later changed to Bronwsboro.

Today the area of Brownsboro still exists, but the stores and the school are long gone. Pictured is the Brownsboro School *circa* 1917.

The town of Derby was located in the Upper Rogue area. The Derby School is pictured.

All that remains of the town of Antelope is the cemetery. Antelope was located near the town of Eagle Point.

6

TABLE ROCK CITY TO ASHLAND MILLS

Not everyone who arrived in Jackson County in the 1850s were pioneers. Some of the earliest settlers in Jackson County came from China. They arrived on American soil, not with the intent of beginning a new life here, but instead to work the gold fields then return home with enough money to be able to provide for their families.

The majority of Chinese immigrants were young men who travelled alone, leaving their wives and children behind. The long journey to a foreign land rife with uncertainties looked much more promising than the reality of staying put where opportunities to make a living were scarce. As one Chinese farmer said:

> I work on four-mou land [less than one acre, a larger-than-average holding] year in and year out, from dawn to dusk, but after taxes and providing for your own needs, I make $20 a year. You make that much in one day. No matter how much it cost to get there, or how hard the work is, America is still better than this.

The Chinese who set out in the 1850s, traveled by sailing ships that could take three months or more at sea. The 1860s saw the advent of the Trans-Pacific steamship which shortened the time to approximately forty-five days. Either way, the journey was excruciatingly difficult. The men were crammed into close quarters for the long and arduous journey. Once they arrived on American soil, they were met by a manager who worked for an association based in China. The men had no option but to go to work for the association, as they were not allowed to own a mining claim on their own and could only work for an association. The association would decide where to send the new arrivals based on what contracts they had with the miners. Many of them were brought to Jackson County to work in the gold mines.

An early day photograph of Table Rock City. The name of the town was later changed to Jacksonville.

Today nothing is left of the Chinatown that was located on present day Main Street in Jacksonville. Pictured is a Chinese New Year's celebration in Jacksonville's Chinatown. Chinese New Year was one of the few times that the pioneers mingled with the Chinese, who otherwise were distrusted and discriminated against.

Kanaka Flats was located a mile-and-a-half outside of Jacksonville. It was home to minorities who were not welcome in the nearby towns. The last of the Kanaka Flats community members left the area decades ago. Today, Kanaka Flats Road leads to homes tucked into the hills.

Today Fern Valley Road is a busy thoroughfare, but the town of Fern Valley is just a distant memory. Pictured is the Fern Valley School *circa* 1913. Miss Hopper is on the left with Miss Miller on the right. The students, from left to right, are Ethel Alford, Mildred Hughes, Mildred Werl, Echo Alford, Flora ?, Clyde Peast, ?, and Clifford Peast.

The original name of Phoenix was Gasburg. It is thought that the town was given this name due to a very talkative, AKA gassy, young woman named Kate Clayton. Kate worked as a cook when there were just a few settlers in the area. They referred to her as gassy Kate due to her nonstop talking. Main street is pictured looking north.

Another early name for the town of Phoenix was Eden Precinct. This name was selected for the abundance of good agriculture land and the sheer beauty of the area. Early day Main Street looking south is pictured.

Eventually the name of Phoenix was selected for the town.

Samuel and Huldah Colver were some of the first settlers to the town that would eventually be named Phoenix. They took out a Donation Land Claim for 640 acres and began farming.

The Colvers built a small cabin which was replaced by this house in the late 1850s. The house served as a community gathering place for meetings, dances, and meals. In 1879, Abigail Scott Duniway delivered an address on woman's suffragette at the house.

Samuel died in a snowstorm in Klamath County in February 1891. Huldah died in Phoenix in August 1907. The Colver house remained in the family until 1923. It served many purposes in the ensuing decades, including a private home, hotel, restaurant, museum, and antique store. The Colver House succumbed to a fire in 2008. The picture above shows the house after the fire and before it was bulldozed.

The town of Talent was originally known as Wagner or Wagner Creek. Jacob Wagner was an early settler to the area. He took out a Donation Land Claim and began farming. Eventually Aaron Talent bought the land from Wagner. He became the town's postmaster and renamed the town Talent.

The original name of Ashland was Ashland Mills. Abel Helman and Eber Emery were some of the first to settle in the area. They built a water powered sawmill and named the town Ashland Mills. The name was later shortened to Ashland.

7

ABANDONED MODES OF TRANSPORTATION

An early photograph of covered wagons.

Rare photographs of early day stagecoaches are pictured.

Stagecoaches paid anywhere from $40 to $80 to cross a toll bridge such as the one pictured. Those on horseback or walking paid 25 cents.

Opposite page:

Above: Barron's Station is pictured when it was a stage stop high up in the mountains outside of Ashland. It was built for Hugh Barron and was one of the first frame structure houses in Jackson County. There were sixty stage stops between Sacramento and Portland. A one-way trip took seven days to complete.

Below: Josiah and Hattie Beeman are pictured with their horse in front of their home at 504 1st Ave in Gold Hill. When they built the home in 1901, it was the first home in Gold Hill to have indoor plumbing. Josiah leased and later purchased the Lucky Bart Mine, which was located on Sardine Creek. In 1993, the Beeman family left the house to the Gold Hill Historical Society so that it could be used as a museum.

John Black operated this ferry across the Rogue River near Shady Cove from 1891-1895.

The pioneers who arrived in Jackson County saw many changes during their lifetime. Just in transportation, they experienced covered wagons, stagecoaches, the advent of the railroad, the invention of the automobile, and some even saw the airplane pictured above that flew into Medford on June 4, 1910.

ABOUT THE AUTHOR

Historian Margaret LaPlante lives in southern Oregon. She has written many books, magazine articles, and short stories on the history of Oregon.